GRADE

03
DRUMS

Published by
Trinity College London Press Ltd
trinitycollege.com

Registered in England
Company no. 09726123

Photography by Zute Lightfoot, lightfootphoto.com

© Copyright 2017 Trinity College London Press Ltd
Sixth impression, January 2024

Printed in England by Halstan & Co Ltd, Amersham, Bucks

Parental and Teacher Guidance:

The songs in Trinity's Rock & Pop syllabus have been arranged
to represent the artists' original recordings as closely and
authentically as possible. Popular music frequently deals with
subject matter that some may find offensive or challenging.
It is possible that the songs may include material that some
might find unsuitable for use with younger learners.

We recommend that parents and teachers exercise their own
judgement to satisfy themselves that the lyrics of selected
songs are appropriate for the students concerned. As you
will be aware, there is no requirement that all songs in this
syllabus must be learned. Trinity does not associate itself with,
adopt or endorse any of the opinions or views expressed in
the selected songs.

THE EXAM AT A GLANCE

In your exam you will perform a set of three songs and one of the session skills assessments. You can choose the order of your set list.

SONG 1

Choose a song from this book.

SONG 2

Choose *either* a different song from this book
or a song from the list of additional Trinity Rock & Pop arrangements, available at trinityrock.com
or a song you have chosen yourself: this could be your own cover version or a song that you have written. It should be at the same level as the songs in this book and match the parameters at trinityrock.com

SONG 3: TECHNICAL FOCUS

Song 3 is designed to help you develop specific and relevant techniques in performance. Choose one of the technical focus songs from this book, which cover two specific technical elements.

SESSION SKILLS

Choose *either* **playback** *or* **improvising**.

Session skills are an essential part of every Rock & Pop exam. They are designed to help you develop the techniques music industry performers need.

Sample tests are available in our *Session Skills* books and free examples can be downloaded from trinityrock.com

ACCESS ALL AREAS

GET THE FULL ROCK & POP EXPERIENCE ONLINE AT TRINITYROCK.COM

We have created a range of digital resources to support your learning and give you insider information from the music industry, available online. You will find support, advice and digital content on:

- Songs, performance and technique
- Session skills
- The music industry

You can access tips and tricks from industry professionals featuring:

- Bite-sized videos that include tips from professional musicians on techniques used in the songs
- 'Producer's notes' on the tracks, to increase your knowledge of rock and pop
- Blog posts on performance tips, musical styles, developing technique and advice from the music industry

JOIN US ONLINE AT:

 /TRINITYROCKANDPOP    @TRINITY_ROCK    /TRINITYROCKANDPOP   and at TRINITYROCK.COM

CONTENTS

THE AUDIO

Professional demo & backing tracks can be downloaded free, see inside cover for details.

Music preparation and book layout by Andrew Skirrow for Camden Music Services
Music consultants: Nick Crispin, Chris Walters, Christopher Hussey, James Sedge
Audio arranged, recorded & produced by Tom Fleming
Drum arrangements by George Double

Musicians
Bass: Tom Fleming, Sam Burgess
Drums: George Double
Guitar: Tom Fleming
Vocals: Bo Walton, Alison Symons, Brendan Reilly

DRUM LEGEND

Drum kit notation can vary between different publishers and arrangers. The key below is used throughout this series and is becoming more consistently used.

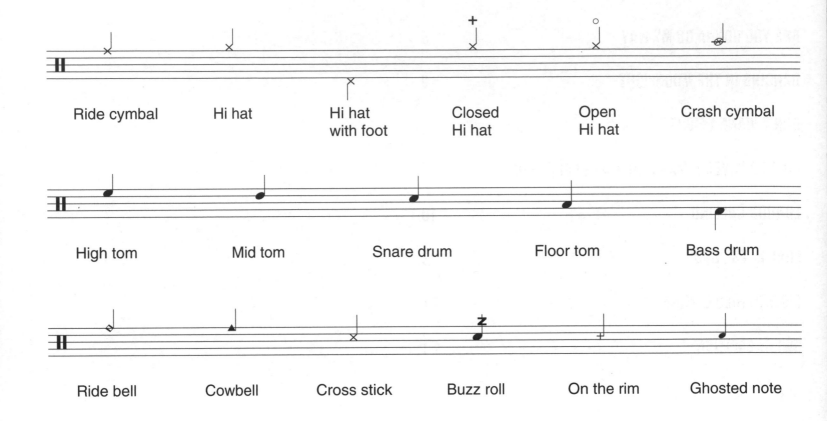

| Ride cymbal | Hi hat | Hi hat with foot | Closed Hi hat | Open Hi hat | Crash cymbal |

| High tom | Mid tom | Snare drum | Floor tom | Bass drum |

| Ride bell | Cowbell | Cross stick | Buzz roll | On the rim | Ghosted note |

TECHNICAL FOCUS

ARE YOU GONNA GO MY WAY

LENNY KRAVITZ

WORDS AND MUSIC: LENNY KRAVITZ, CRAIG ROSS

SINGLE BY
Lenny Kravitz

ALBUM
Are You Gonna Go My Way

B-SIDE
**It Ain't Over 'Til It's Over
Always on The Run
Let Love Rule
My Love
All My Life
Someone Like You**

RELEASED
22 February 1993

RECORDED
**1992, Waterfront Studios
Hoboken, New Jersey, USA**

LABEL
Virgin

WRITERS
**Lenny Kravitz
Craig Ross**

PRODUCER
Lenny Kravitz

New York-born Lenny Kravitz is a singer, songwriter, multi-instrumentalist and producer who has released 11 albums since 1989. As well as scoring big hits such as 'It Ain't Over 'Til It's Over' and 'Fly Away', he has also co-written and produced hit singles for Madonna ('Justify My Love') and Vanessa Paradis ('Be My Baby').

The title track and lead single from his third album, the Hendrix-like 'Are You Gonna Go My Way', helped secure Kravitz his first top-20 album in the US and his first No. 1 album both in the UK and Australia, achieving worldwide sales of over four million. Released in February 1993, this classic rock anthem reached No. 4 in the UK and No. 1 in Australia. The song was co-written by Kravitz with guitarist Craig Ross, who had joined Kravitz's band for the tour to promote his 1991 album *Mama Said*. Kravitz said:

> It was one of those songs that happened in five minutes. We were jamming. I thought there was something happening. I told Henry [Hirsch, engineer and keyboard player] to turn the tape machines on, and we played it. And that was it.

Ross played all the guitar parts on the recording, Kravitz taking on the role of drummer.

TECHNICAL FOCUS

Two technical focus elements are featured in this song:

- Flams
- Rhythm

This song strongly features **flams** right from the start. The challenge is to get these sounding absolutely consistent, and to replicate this when the flams come back at 39. There are also challenging moments of **rhythm**, in particular bar 28 which needs to be played exactly as written in order to sync with the backing track.

TECHNICAL FOCUS

ARE YOU GONNA GO MY WAY

WORDS AND MUSIC:
LENNY KRAVITZ, CRAIG ROSS

SINGLE BY
Toploader

ALBUM
Onka's Big Moka

B-SIDE
**Dancing in the Moonlight
(Stargate Radio Mix)**

**Dancing in the Moonlight
(Alliance DC Vocal Remix)**

**Dancing in the Moonlight
(Live)**

RELEASED
February 2000

RECORDED
1999

LABEL
**S2
Epic**

WRITER
Sherman Kelly

PRODUCER
George Drakoulias

DANCING IN THE MOONLIGHT

TOPLOADER

WORDS AND MUSIC: SHERMAN KELLY

Hailing from the coastal town of Eastbourne in England, Toploader hit big with their million-selling debut album in 1999. The band are Joseph Washbourn (vocals/keyboard and songwriter), Julian Deane (lead guitar), Dan Hipgrave (rhythm guitar), Matt Knight (bass) and Rob Green (drums).

Toploader originally released 'Dancing in the Moonlight' as a single in February 2000, where it reached a UK peak of No. 19. Following the top-five success of their debut album *Onka's Big Moka* that summer, the song was re-released in November that year. This time it became the band's biggest and most enduring hit, reaching No. 7 in the UK and going platinum after spending 25 weeks in the charts.
The song is by the band King Harvest, formed in 1970 in Paris, France, by four American expatriates. Keyboard player Sherman Kelly wrote the song in 1968, and King Harvest released it as a single four years later, earning them 'one-hit wonder' status as the song became their sole hit after reaching No. 13 in the US.

 ## PERFORMANCE TIPS

The first-time bar and chorus both have an off-beat skipped snare drum part which adds a nice funky feel to this song. You might want to learn each individual 'snare skip' separately before putting them together.

DANCING IN THE MOONLIGHT

WORDS AND MUSIC: SHERMAN KELLY

DON'T WANNA FIGHT
ALABAMA SHAKES

WORDS AND MUSIC: ALABAMA SHAKES

SINGLE BY
Alabama Shakes

ALBUM
Sound & Color

RELEASED
10 February 2015

LABEL
ATO (USA)
Rough Trade (UK)

WRITER
Alabama Shakes

PRODUCER
Blake Mills

Alabama Shakes formed in 2009 with a blend of fiery blues-rock and hard-hitting Southern soul, quickly bringing them international attention. With a formidable live reputation and two hit albums they have become one of the biggest bands to emerge in the 2010s.

'Don't Wanna Fight' was the first taste of Alabama Shakes' second album, 2015's US chart-topper *Sound & Color*. An electrifying mix of funky guitar riffs, soulful bass, chunky drums and the passionately raspy vocal performance of singer Brittany Howard, the impressive track expanded the band's range into more diverse, genre-bending territory. Likening the singer's opening howl to a hurricane, *Rolling Stone* magazine wrote, 'After reintroducing herself with a spine-tingling squeal, singer-guitarist Brittany Howard goes on to deliver a dizzying vocal performance that splits the difference between James Brown and Barry Gibb.' The song received two Grammy Awards in February 2016 for Best Rock Song and Best Rock Performance, with *Sound & Color* also picking up the Best Alternative Music Album honour.

⚡ PERFORMANCE TIPS

The verse features syncopated snare drum and bass drum notes. Take care to place these accurately – subdividing as you count the beat will help. This is the most technically challenging section, but the rest of the song requires stamina and an energetic, driving feel. Look out for the change of groove at bar 46.

DON'T WANNA FIGHT

WORDS AND MUSIC: ALABAMA SHAKES

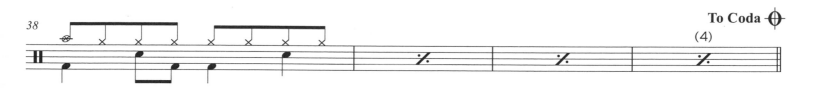

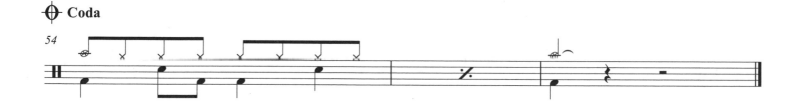

YOUR
PAGE
NOTES

SINGLE BY
Aretha Franklin

ALBUM
**I Never Loved a Man the
Way I Love You**

B-SIDE
**Do Right Woman, Do
Right Man**

RELEASED
10 March 1967 (album)

RECORDED
24 January 1967

LABEL
Atlantic

WRITER
Ronnie Shannon

PRODUCER
Jerry Wexler

TECHNICAL FOCUS

I NEVER LOVED A MAN (THE WAY I LOVE YOU) ARETHA FRANKLIN

WORDS AND MUSIC: RONNIE SHANNON

Born in Memphis, Tennessee in 1942, Aretha Franklin grew up singing gospel in her father's church before signing her first record deal at the age of 18. The first female performer to be inducted into the Rock and Roll Hall of Fame, a 2010 poll by *Rolling Stone* magazine placed her at No. 1 in the 100 Greatest Singers of All Time.

Aretha Franklin recorded nine albums for Columbia Records between 1960 and 1966. Jerry Wexler signed her to Atlantic Records in 1967 and arranged for her to record with an all-white group of Southern session musicians called the Muscle Shoals Rhythm Section, who had played on Percy Sledge's 'When a Man Loves a Woman' and Wilson Pickett's 'Mustang Sally'. Written specifically for Franklin by songwriter Ronnie Shannon, 'I Never Loved a Man (The Way I Love You)' was released as Franklin's debut single with the label and it became her first top-ten hit (as well as topping the US R&B chart for seven weeks). It also provided Franklin with the title of her tenth album, widely regarded as an all-time classic album and one that established the singer as 'The Queen of Soul'.

TECHNICAL FOCUS

Two technical focus elements are featured in this song:

- Slow shuffle feel
- Double-stopped crescendo

This song features a **slow shuffle feel** in $\frac{3}{4}$ time. The challenge is to keep this light and bouncy, relaxed at all times and avoiding heaviness. The **double-stopped crescendo** in bars 41–42 is played with the snare and floor tom together. Keep this tight and controlled (no flamming) with an even crescendo in into bar 43.

I NEVER LOVED A MAN (THE WAY I LOVE YOU)

WORDS AND MUSIC: RONNIE SHANNON

YOUR
PAGE
NOTES

LONDON CALLING

THE CLASH

WORDS AND MUSIC: JOE STRUMMER, MICK JONES

SINGLE BY
The Clash

ALBUM
London Calling

B-SIDE
Armagideon Time

RELEASED
7 December 1979

RECORDED
**August, September &
November 1979
Wessex Studios
London, England**

LABEL
Epic

WRITERS
**Joe Strummer
Mick Jones**

PRODUCER
Guy Stevens

Formed in London, England, in 1976, The Clash were one of the most politically motivated and seminal bands of the UK punk scene and by 1978 comprised Joe Strummer (vocals, guitar), Mick Jones (vocals, guitar), Paul Simonon (bass) and Topper Headon (drums). All six of the band's studio albums, and 11 albums in total, reached the UK top 20.

Named after the call signal of the BBC's World Service broadcasts, 'London Calling' was the title track and only UK single from The Clash's third album. Released at the end of 1979, the single reached No. 11 in the UK with the album reaching No. 9. The double album also marked the band's commercial breakthrough in the US, and *Rolling Stone* magazine would later rank *London Calling* at No. 1 in their best albums of the 80s poll, describing it as

> An emergency broadcast from rock's last angry band ... skidding between ska, reggae, R&B, third-world music, power pop and full-tilt punk, the Clash stormed the gates of rock convention and single-handedly set the agenda – musically, politically and emotionally – for the decade to come.

Clash fans Bob Dylan and Bruce Springsteen have both performed the album's title track in concert on more than one occasion.

⚡ PERFORMANCE TIPS

This song has an angry energy that you should do your best to capture – but try to do this through controlled intensity rather than uncontrolled loudness. There is a lot of variety between sections, requiring precision, and the flammed triplets in the breakdown section will need to be practised for rhythmic accuracy. You may wish to subdivide your counting of these bars into triplet quavers, counting two of these for each triplet crotchet.

LONDON CALLING

WORDS AND MUSIC:

JOE STRUMMER, MICK JONES

YOUR
PAGE
NOTES

LOVE IS THE DRUG
ROXY MUSIC

WORDS AND MUSIC: BRYAN FERRY, ANDY MACKAY

SINGLE BY
Roxy Music

ALBUM
Siren

B-SIDE
Sultanesque

RELEASED
September 1975

RECORDED
Summer 1975

LABEL
EG

WRITERS
Bryan Ferry
Andy Mackay

PRODUCER
Chris Thomas

Roxy Music were a hugely influential and commercially successful art rock band who made an instant impact with their debut single 'Virginia Plain' in 1972 at the onset of glam rock mania. Fronted by Bryan Ferry and initially featuring Brian Eno on synthesizer, Roxy Music produced ten UK hit singles over the next decade.

Written by Roxy Music's saxophone and oboe player Andy Mackay with lyrics and vocal line by Ferry, 'Love Is the Drug' was the lead single and opening track on the band's fifth album, 1975's *Siren*. The single reached No. 2 in the UK (kept off the top spot by a reissue of David Bowie's 'Space Oddity') and was also the band's first (and biggest) hit in the US. Grace Jones covered the song for her 1980 *Warm Leatherette* album, and Ferry later reinterpreted the song in a 1920s jazz style for the soundtrack to Baz Luhrmann's 2013 film *The Great Gatsby*.

⚡ PERFORMANCE TIPS

The hi hat being opened on beat 4 at the same time as the snare drum is an interesting feature of this song. Be sure to keep the hi hat open for the whole crotchet until the first beat of the next bar. The 'ending' section goes into a half-time feel by moving the snare to beat 3. This should have the effect of making the music seem more spacious and relaxed.

LOVE IS THE DRUG

WORDS AND MUSIC:
BRYAN FERRY, ANDY MACKAY

Intro

Rock ♩ = **124** (1½ bars count-in)
Snares off

Verse

YOUR
PAGE
NOTES

TECHNICAL FOCUS

SWEET CHILD O' MINE
GUNS N' ROSES

WORDS AND MUSIC: AXL ROSE, SLASH, IZZY STRADLIN
DUFF MCKAGAN, STEVEN ADLER

SINGLE BY
Guns N' Roses

ALBUM
Appetite for Destruction

B-SIDE
It's So Easy (live)
Out Ta Get Me

RELEASED
21 July 1987 (album)
17 August 1988 (single)

RECORDED
March–April 1987

Rumbo Studios, Canoga Park, California, USA

Take One Studio, Burbank, California, USA

The Record Plant, Los Angeles, California, USA

Can-Am Studios, Tarzana, California, USA (album)

LABEL
Geffen

WRITERS
Axl Rose, Slash
Izzy Stradlin
Duff McKagan
Steven Adler

PRODUCER
Mike Clink

Formed in LA in 1985, Guns N' Roses are an American rock group who became one of the world's biggest bands by the end of the decade. Going through various incarnations over the years, the best-known line-up comprises vocalist Axl Rose, lead guitarist Slash, rhythm guitarist Izzy Stradlin, bassist Duff McKagan and drummer Steven Adler.

'Sweet Child o' Mine' was released as a single in August 1988 and reached No. 1 in the US the following month, renewing interest in the band's debut album *Appetite for Destruction* which had been released more than a year earlier. By the end of the year, the album had sold three million copies worldwide. To date it has sold more than 30 million copies, making it one of the biggest-selling albums ever released and the best-selling debut in US history. Not all members of the band are fans of their biggest hit.

It was like a joke,' said McKagan. 'We thought, what is this song? It's gonna be nothing.

Slash commented: I hated it for years, but it would cause such a reaction. Just playing the first stupid notes used to evoke this hysteria, so I've finally gotten to appreciate it.

TECHNICAL FOCUS

Two technical focus elements are featured in this song:

- Pushes
- Triplet flams

In the chorus, take care with the placement of the crashes which come on the first beat and halfway through the second beat. The latter are called **pushes**. You may want to count through them until you are comfortable with the rhythm. The song ends with a bar of crotchet **triplet flams** – you will need to practise keeping the pulse consistent as you play this completely new rhythm.

TECHNICAL FOCUS

SWEET CHILD O' MINE

WORDS AND MUSIC:
AXL ROSE, SLASH, IZZY STRADLIN
DUFF MCKAGAN, STEVEN ADLER

YOUR
PAGE
NOTES

SWEET EMOTION AEROSMITH

WORDS AND MUSIC: STEVEN TYLER, TOM HAMILTON

Please note: This song contains subject matter that some might find inappropriate for younger learners. Please refer to the Parental and Teacher Guidance at the beginning of this book for more information.

SINGLE BY
Aerosmith

ALBUM
Toys in the Attic

B-SIDE
Uncle Salty

RELEASED
19 May 1975

RECORDED
14 March 1975
New York City
New York, USA

LABEL
Columbia

WRITERS
Steven Tyler
Tom Hamilton

PRODUCER
Jack Douglas

American rock band Aerosmith formed in Boston, Massachusetts, in 1970, and by the following year comprised Steven Tyler (vocals), Joe Perry (guitar), Brad Whitford (guitar), Tom Hamilton (bass) and Joey Kramer (drums). They are the best-selling American heavy rock band in music history with worldwide sales of over 150 million, almost half of that in the US alone.

Towards the end of sessions for Aerosmith's third album, 1975's *Toys in the Attic*, producer Jack Douglas asked the band for any additional musical ideas they might have. Bassist Hamilton dusted off a riff he had been playing with for several years, inspired by Jeff Beck's 1969 instrumental track 'Rice Pudding'. After presenting an arrangement to the band, 'Steven took the intro, turned it around, changed key, and we used it as the tag, the resolution of the song,' Hamilton explained. 'Brad, Joey and I went home. Next time we heard "Sweet Emotion" it had the overdubs, the vocals, and I flipped out. I loved what they did with it.'

⚡ PERFORMANCE TIPS

Keep both your feet on the pedals for the open hi hats that are played simultaneously with the bass drum, starting at bar 9. Riff 2 features some double-handed hi hat playing, requiring precision. The semiquavers on the hi hat should run smoothly and evenly into the semiquavers on the snare at the end of each bar.

SWEET EMOTION

WORDS AND MUSIC:
STEVEN TYLER, TOM HAMILTON

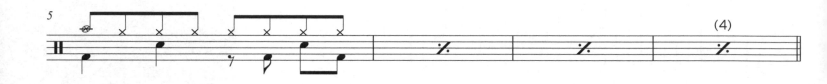

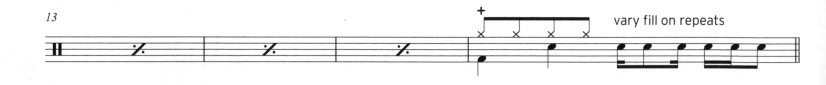

vary fill on repeats

Coda

Riff 2

Guitar solo

FILL around kit

YOUR
PAGE
NOTES

PLAYING WITH BACKING TRACKS

All your backing tracks can be downloaded from soundwise.co.uk

- The backing tracks begin with a click track, which sets the tempo and helps you start accurately

- Be careful to balance the volume of the backing track against your instrument

- Listen carefully to the backing track to ensure that you are playing in time

If you are creating your own backing track, here are some further tips:

- Make sure that the sound quality is of a good standard

- Think carefully about the instruments/sounds you are using on the backing track

- Avoid copying what you are playing in the exam on the backing track – it should support, not duplicate

- Do you need to include a click track at the beginning?

COPYRIGHT IN A SONG

If you are a singer, instrumentalist or songwriter it is important to know about copyright. When someone writes a song they automatically own the copyright (sometimes called 'the rights'). Copyright begins once a piece of music has been documented or recorded (eg by video, CD or score notation) and protects the interests of the creators. This means that others cannot copy it, sell it, make it available online or record it without the owner's permission or the appropriate licence.

COVER VERSIONS

- When an artist creates a new version of a song it is called a 'cover version'

- The majority of songwriters subscribe to licensing agencies, also known as 'collecting societies'. When a songwriter is a member of such an agency, the performing rights to their material are transferred to the agency (this includes cover versions of their songs)

- The agency works on the writer's behalf by issuing licences to performance venues, who report what songs have been played, which in turn means that the songwriter will receive a payment for any songs used

- You can create a cover version of a song and use it in an exam without needing a licence

There are different rules for broadcasting (eg TV, radio, internet), selling or copying (pressing CDs, DVDs etc), and for printed material, and the appropriate licences should be sought out.

CHOOSING SONGS FOR YOUR EXAM

SONG 1

Choose a song from this book.

SONG 2

Choose a song which is:

Either a different song from this book

or from the list of additional Trinity Rock & Pop arrangements, available at trinityrock.com

or from a printed or online source

or your own arrangement

or a song that you have written yourself

You can play Song 2 unaccompanied or with a backing track (minus the drum part). If you like, you can create a backing track yourself (or with friends), add your own vocals, or be accompanied live by another musician.

The level of difficulty and length of the song should be similar to the songs in this book and match the parameters available at trinityrock.com

When choosing a song, think about:

- Does it work on my instrument?

- Are there any technical elements that are too difficult for me? (If so, perhaps save it for when you do the next grade)

- Do I enjoy playing it?

- Does it work with my other songs to create a good set list?

SONG 3: TECHNICAL FOCUS

Song 3 is designed to help you develop specific and relevant techniques in performance. Choose one of the technical focus songs from this book, which cover two specific technical elements.

SHEET MUSIC

If your choice for Song 2 is not from this book, you must provide the examiner with a photocopy. The title, writers of the song and your name should be on the sheet music. You must also bring an original copy of the book, or a download version with proof of purchase, for each song that you perform in the exam.

Your music can be:

- A lead sheet with lyrics, chords and melody line

- A chord chart with lyrics

- A full score using conventional staff notation